The Power

by

Jerry Hopkins, Jr.

The Power of Gratitude
by Jerry Hopkins, Jr.

September 2005

All Rights Reserved
Copyright 2005 Jerry Hopkins, Jr.

Published by Hopkins Business Services, Inc. 5314 Yosemite Dr., Medina, OH 44256

Cover Design by Tohamas Brewster

www.thepowerofgratitude.com

No part of this book may be reproduced or transmitted in any form or by any means, electronic or mechanical, including photo copying, recording, or by any information storage and retrieval system, without permission in writing from the publisher.

Copyright 2005 Jerry Hopkins, Jr.

Printing History:
September, 2005 First Edition

Table of Contents

Preface 6
- How Gratitude Changed My Life 6
- How I learned about the Power Of Gratitude 7
- What will The Power of Gratitude do for you? 8

Acknowledgments 10

Introduction 11

SECTION I: The Source of Gratitude 16
- Gratitude is emphasized in the Bible 17
- According to the Bible, gratitude is a good thing 21
- So, when should we give thanks? 22
- What should I be thankful for? 23
- Noah gives thanks 24

SECTION II: Expressing Gratitude 25
- Tithing 25
- The story of Job 26
- My story 27

SECTION III: What Others Say About Gratitude 32
- Books on success that talk about gratitude 32

SECTION IV: Gratitude and Business Success 38
- Giving thanks in advance 43
- Thanking Customers 43
- Real gratitude can give you an edge over your competition 44
- Adding use value to your product or service 46
- Thanking Employees 47
- Employee to employee gratitude 47

SECTION V: How to Show Gratitude 49
- Mistakes 50
- Visualization is the key 51
- One of the secrets to prayer is that gratitude is said first 52
- The secret to gratitude is the sincere feeling you put into it 54

SECTION VI: The Gratitude Prayer 55
- Visualization for The Gratitude Prayer 57
- When to Say the Gratitude Prayer 57

Final Thoughts 60

Preface

"In everything give thanks, for this is the will of God ..."
1 Thessalonians 5:18

How Gratitude Changed My Life

Thank you for reading this book.

Yes, I really mean that. You see, the two magic words "thank you" will change your life instantly, like it has changed mine. But you might ask yourself, how can two simple words change my life, especially since these words are tossed around willy-nilly everyday? Well, it's not just the words. Words are nothing more than icons for thoughts and feelings. What I am talking about is permanent change from within -- changing your thoughts and feelings from negative to positive. This kind of life-altering change can only be accomplished through gratitude.

Please let me explain:

I went through most of my early life angry -- mad that I didn't have rich parents, that I didn't get lucky, or that I didn't have all the things that I wanted. I deserved them and damn it, the world owed them to me.

Does this sound like you?

- You are mad that you have not yet received all the riches and opportunity you believe rightfully belong to you.
- You are not where you should be in life.

- You are confused has to why you are not happy.
- You wonder why your prayers are not being answered.

If you answered "yes, that's me!" to even one of the above statements, then this might be the most important book you will read in your entire life.

How I learned about the Power of Gratitude

Those who are not where they want to be life are lagging behind because they are missing an important link -- gratitude. That's right, if you understand how to properly use gratitude, your life will change and you will reach previously unimaginable success.

Before I discovered the importance of gratitude, it didn't seem to matter how hard I worked or what I did. Nothing changed in my life despite my efforts and I began to get bitter. The more I spinned my wheels, the more bitter I became. That is, until something magical happened.

Several years ago my mother was diagnosed with cancer. She also had other health issues, the most severe of which was her failing kidneys. When we took her to the hospital, the doctors told us that her kidneys could no longer function and that she was going to die. I was able to spend that last week with her. Now, my mom wasn't a great philosopher or anything, yet in those last few days, she taught me a lot about living. Even though the lessons were hard, I was grateful for them.

I still wonder in amazement, that in just a few days time, I experienced the most significant moments of my life as I immersed myself in a "suddenly" loving relationship with my mother. Yes, those last few days were hard -- very hard. Yet remarkably, they were among the most beautiful experiences of my life.

I miss my mom, but she taught me a valuable lesson that I will never forget.

I decided to turn my life around

I wouldn't be telling you this if it wasn't important. Clearly, it's easy to be grateful for the good things in your life, but it is difficult to be grateful when bad things happen. However, there is always a reason for events to happen the way they do, or for lessons to be learned the way they are. There was a lesson for my mom and for me. Through this lesson, my gratitude toward God and other people was awakened and my life became fuller, richer, and more wonderful. I would now like to pass this lesson on to you.

It takes a very special person to appreciate the law of gratitude. The soul that is always grateful lives in closer touch with God than the one that never looks to him in thankful acknowledgment. That's why I don't believe that you are reading this book by accident.

What will The Power Of Gratitude do for you?

It will help you to do the following:

- Teach you the hows and whys of the gratitude. It's not just about thinking positive. Learn the real secret behind it.
- Lose the fear of living. Most people live their lives in fear. That's why they don't have the life they want.
- Learn how to work gratitude into your prayer life.
- Learn to turn emotional blows into positive life-changing events.
- Improve your relationship with your spouse and children.
- Turn fear into confidence.
- Become more prosperous.

Why suffer with an unproductive life? Just think how much easier your life will be when you put *The Power of Gratitude* program to work for you.

Sincerely,

Jerry Hopkins

Acknowledgments

What would a course on gratitude be without saying thanks to the ones who have helped me to reach my dreams of success?

Of course, the first one to thank is God. Without God, I wouldn't be here and wouldn't have learned the lessons that I needed to advance spiritually, physically, and mentally. He is the reason that I am a success.

The next person I would like to thank is my mom. Mom, you will forever be in my heart and you will not ever be forgotten. I thank you for the valuable lessons that you taught me. This course is dedicated to you.

Like a lot of successful people, I stand on the shoulders of giants. One of those giants is Matt Furey. I owe a lot to Matt, who helped me believe in myself. He helped me to refine my gratitude and encouraged me to create this course.

I would also like to thank Guy Savelli, who gave me the gift, The Sincerity Prayer, and taught me that we all have the gift of life inside us.

Special thanks goes to Tohamas Brewster who created the most beautiful illustrations that go along with this book.

The grateful mind is constantly fixed upon the best; therefore it tends to become the best; it takes the form of character of the best, and will receive the best.
Wallace Wattles

Introduction

You might be asking yourself, "why a program for gratitude?" After all, you may think that you are already grateful. But, like a lot of things we do in modern society, many of us actually just go through the motions of gratitude. We say the words and don't put much thought into them, let alone emotion. Have you ever done something special for someone and when they say "thanks," you feel let down? Why would this happen? It happens because you know they just said "thanks," but didn't mean it -- they weren't really grateful for what you did, they said "thanks" as a common courtesy.

So, how do you think others feel when you just say "thanks" in passing, if you even give thanks at all. What about God, do you thank God with sincerity? Do you really believe that God will give you more when you haven't even given him thanks for what he has already given to you?

The concept of gratitude may seem simplistic. We are used to things that are complex -- that are at times, difficult to figure out. But, the fact is that the simpler something is, the more likely it is that it will work. If what you're doing now isn't working for you, why not try something that will?

You may be thinking, I thought this program was about success, not some sort of religious lesson. Well, let me tell you that some of the most successful people in the world are very religious.

Real success is achievement in your business life AND your personal life

If you study, like I have, all the great books on success, you will find the above common theme. This is a different way to use your mind. Most people think books on success should be "how to" manuals. They look for books on topics like, how to start a company, the laws of business, how to set up a web site, how to make products, etc. In other words, most people want to know the mechanics of starting and running a business. And while these things are important, people get too hung up on them.

I have known people who have started businesses and failed because they spent too much of their time and energy on the practical side of business. They never really understood why they didn't have success and so they continued to spend more and more time on the practical matters that were getting them nowhere. In fact, when you talk to some of these people, they seem to know a lot about business yet they are not terribly successful.

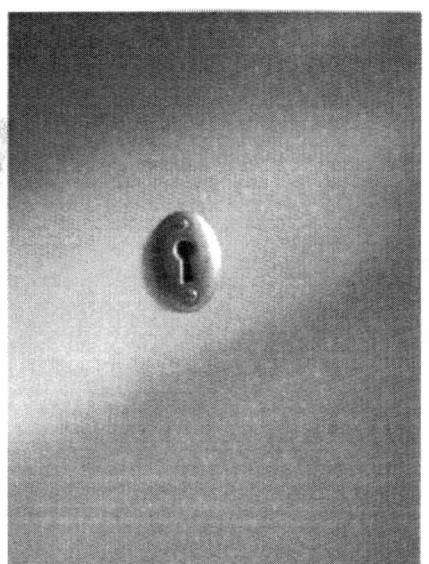

This guide is based on the classic book, *The Science of Getting Rich,* and on my own experiences. *The Science of Getting Rich,* written by Wallace D. Wattles, was published in 1910 and became an instant success thanks to its revolutionary, but extremely do-able, approach to earning money and amassing wealth. In the preface to his book, Wattles writes:

This book is pragmatical, not philosophical; a practical manual, not a treatise upon theories. It is intended for the men and women whose most pressing need is for money; who wish to get rich first, and philosophize afterward. It is for those who have, so far, found neither the time, the means, nor the opportunity to go deeply into the study of metaphysics, but who want results and who are willing to take the conclusions of science as a basis for action, without going into all the processes by which those conclusions were reached.

Don't get me wrong, we are not just talking about getting rich, but about reaching success in all areas in your life. Some of this is going to sound esoteric to the more practical types and some of this will be familiar to others.

I'm sure that a lot of you have read books and have listened to CD's on success. Some of you may have found some success and may be looking to rise to the next level. Success may have eluded others. This program will bring to light the missing success link, gratitude, to those at all levels of business success and also to those who have not yet found it within their grasp.

Now, for those of you who are practical business types, some of the concepts in this course may sound foreign to you. For instance, what does gratitude and prayer have to do with success in business? Well, a lot. It's about your attitude. It's about your employees, contractors, and customers. If you aren't grateful towards them, how long do you think they will stick with you? Not long. Have you ever worked for an ungrateful boss? Did you work hard for them? How long did you work for them? You probably looked for a new job as soon as you could. If you are in the position now, you are probably looking for a way out.

Plenty can be learned by studying those who are successful. When you do this, you will find that most of them are grateful and believe in a higher power. If you doubt this, go to the library and check out some of the classic books on success. Read them and if you think they are hogwash, okay fine.

I'm not going to change your mind. However, I believe that you picked up this course because you are having trouble becoming successful or with moving to the next level. I also believe that you have an open mind. I believe that you have already read several books on success and on business, but success still seems to elude you, like it used to elude me.

Gratitude is an understanding that our life is successful because of the help of others

What really is gratitude? It is an understanding that we are not alone in the world and that we often stand on the shoulders of others. Our parents took care of us when we were young, teachers taught us how to read and write, friends help us through sad times and also make us laugh, strangers help us in times of need, our families give us love, our country gives us freedom, and service men and women like firefighters, police, and soldiers protect us. God has given you life. An endless stream of people in your life has given you more than you could ever have given yourself if you were on the planet alone. We need to give thanks to God and to all of these people on a regular basis.

It is easy to be self-centered. I often hear people say they reached success by themselves. When I hear this, I say, "oh really." You fed yourself as a baby and learned to read and write all by yourself? What about your parents, your teachers, or that first person who believed in you, hired you, or loaned you money to start your business. Have you forgotten your customers and your employees? There is not one person in the world who can honestly say that he/she is the only one responsible for his/her success, because you cannot have success without other people and you cannot be a true success without gratitude.

Now, I'm not saying that there aren't people that start off with more of an advantage than others. People who have less of an advantage should be proud of how they have overcome obstacles and people should feel a sense of satisfaction for overcoming critics. As you will see, I sure didn't have a good head start and there were a lot of people who didn't believe in me. However, I didn't do it alone and I am grateful to all those who stood by me and offered their support.

You can not have success without gratitude.

Ungrateful people are not really successful, even if appearances give the impression that they are. Real success is not just about money, it is in having a balanced life. It is about having a family and friends, good health, a spiritually rich life, and being happy in everything you do. Some people have one of these things, or none, or a couple. The truly successful person has them all.

To understand why gratitude is important, think about the times that you went out of your way to do something for someone or how hard you worked at something, only to be told to do something else, or that you didn't do enough and you were never thanked. How did that make you feel? No one likes an ungrateful boss, actors who don't like their fans, or a spouse that takes him/her for granted. Just think how much better the world would be if everyone was grateful.

This program is not about etiquette, on how to write "thank you" notes, or what to say when someone gives you a gift. This guide is going to help you to feel real gratitude and have true meaning behind it.

Gratitude is an ancient law

SECTION I: The Source of Gratitude

Ancient man understood that everything that he needed for his daily living came from a source greater than himself. The Native Americans thanked nature and God whenever they had to hunt or take anything from nature. Tom Brown, Jr. runs a survival school and has written many books on nature observation and tracking. He learned his skills from an old Native American named Stalking Wolf. The following is from his book, *Tom Brown's Field Guide: Living with the Earth.* Brown is talking about Stalking Wolf cutting down a small tree to make a bow.

> *As he did this, [cut down the tree] he always prayed: "I'm sorry, my brother, but I must take your life so that I may live." But the prayer was not just an apology. It was also a thanksgiving and a way of reassuring the tree's spirit that it would be put to good use. It was a way of acknowledging the gift and showing his respect and love for all of Creation.*[1]

And in talking about using anything from the earth:

> *Nothing was wasted, and whatever was made from the offerings of the earth was made with loving care. This was not only for the sake of survival (since a shoddy job should show up in the implement and eventually hurt his own livelihood), but to give thanks for the gift.*[2]

This is common amongst all hunter/gather societies, past and present. They will always be grateful for food and for the tools that they obtain from nature. There is always thanks to God and also to the animal or plant itself.

---

[1] "Tom Brown's Field Guide: Living with the Earth", Tom Brown, Jr. and Brandt Morgan, p.25
[2] "Tom Brown's Field Guide: Living with the Earth", Tom Brown, Jr. and Brandt Morgan, p.25

In Old Testament times, there was great thanksgiving in times of abundant harvest. Hands were lifted up, sacrifices were laid on the alter, and all eyes looked up towards God as they praised him for all that they had been provided by the land that he created.

As the people of the past thanked the heavens for all they had reaped, they were continually given more. These lessons have not been lost in modern times. After all, saying Grace before a meal is offering thanks to God for the meal about to be eaten.

Gratitude is emphasized in the Bible

Gratitude is taught in the Bible. While there aren't any specific commandments that require us to be thankful, there are a lot of lessons -- both obvious and not so obvious. I'm not a biblical scholar, but I bet that gratitude is in the top ten things most mentioned in the Bible. In fact, I didn't get every reference of gratitude from the Bible, because there is so much of it, but I did collect some of the main points and would like to share some of the verses with you. Even if you aren't a Christian, these versus just make sense.

Following, are some references to gratitude in the Bible. There are so many more that I simply can't list them all:

> *... let us offer the sacrifice of praise to God continually, that is, the fruit of our lips giving thanks. Hebrews 13:15*

The above verse is a great reference. First, it says that the fruit of our lips must give thanks to God. Second, it says to do this continually. This is part of the theme of this book.

> *Willingly I will sacrifice to Thee; I will give thanks to Thy name, O Lord, for it is good. Psalms 54:6*
>
> *I will give thanks...with all my heart...*
>
> *Psalms 86:12 (cp. Psalms 9:1; 138:1)*

I found the two above references from Psalms and they both show that it isn't just saying "thanks" that is important, it is being genuine and putting real feeling into your gratefulness that is most important. This is what it means to be grateful from the heart.

> *The Pharisee stood and prayed thus with himself, God, I thank thee, that I am not as other men [are], extortioners, unjust, adulterers, or even as this publican. I fast twice in the week, I give tithes of all that I possess. And the publican, standing afar off, would not lift up so much as [his] eyes unto heaven, but smote upon his breast, saying, God be merciful to me a sinner. I tell you, this man went down to his house justified [rather] than the other: for every one that exalteth himself shall be abased; and he that humbleth himself shall be exalted. Luke 18:11-14*

The above reference from the book of Luke demonstrates the importance of humility -- a key component of genuine gratitude. As you can see, the Pharisee gave thanks to God for the sake of appearance, while the publican humbly admitted to being a sinner, thereby delivering a true and earnest message of thanks to God in an indirect manner.

- *Being thankful is not just a good idea, it is one that is commanded by God. The following versus show the emphasis God places on it:*

- *Offer unto God thanksgiving; and pay thy vows unto the most High. Psalms 50:14*

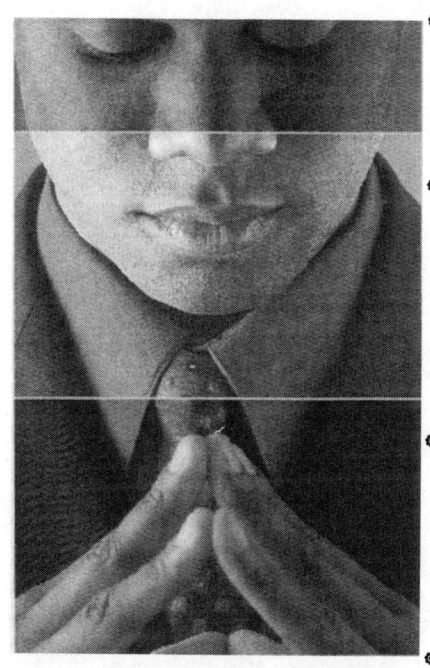

- *Rejoice in the LORD, ye righteous; and give thanks at the remembrance of his holiness. Psalms 97:12*

- *Enter into his gates with thanksgiving, into his courts with praise: be thankful to him, bless his name. Psalms 100:4*

- *Give thanks unto the LORD; call upon his name: make known his deeds among the people. Psalms 105:1*

- *Praise ye the LORD. O give thanks unto the LORD; for [he is] good: for his mercy for ever. Psalms 106:1*

- *Give thanks unto the LORD, for [he is] good: for his mercy for ever. Psalms 107:1*

- *Give thanks unto the LORD; for he is good: for his mercy endureth for ever. Give thanks unto the God of gods: for his mercy endureth for ever. O give thanks to the Lord of lords: for his mercy endureth for ever. Psalms 136:1-3*

- *For this ye know, that no whoremonger, nor unclean person, nor covetous man, who is an idolater, hath any inheritance in the kingdom of Christ and of God. Neither filthiness, nor foolish talking, nor jesting, which are not convenient: but rather giving of thanks. Ephesians 5:3-4, Speaking to yourselves in psalms and hymns and spiritual songs, singing and making melody in your heart to the Lord; Giving thanks always for all things unto God and the Father in the name of our Lord Jesus Christ; Ephesians 5: 19, 20*

- *Giving thanks unto the Father, which hath made us meet to be partakers of the inheritance of the saints in light: Colossians 1:12;*

- *As ye have therefore received Christ Jesus the Lord, [so] walk ye in him: Rooted and built up in him, and established in the faith, as ye have been taught, abounding therein with thanksgiving. Colossians 2:6-7*

- *And let the peace of God rule in your hearts, to which also ye are called in one body; and be ye thankful. Let the word of Christ dwell in you richly in all wisdom; teaching and admonishing one another in psalms and hymns and spiritual songs, singing with grace in your hearts to the Lord. And whatsoever ye do in word or deed, [do] all in the name of the Lord Jesus, giving thanks to God and the Father by him. Colossians 3:15-17*

- *Continue in prayer, and watch in the same with thanksgiving; Colossians 4:2*

- *In every thing give thanks: for this is the will of God in Christ Jesus concerning you. 1 Thessalonians 5:18*

- *I exhort therefore, that, first of all, supplications, prayers, intercessions, [and] giving of thanks, be made for all men; 1 Timothy 2:1*

Jesus also was a leading example of showing gratitude. Throughout the

New Testament, he is almost always giving thanks to God. Below, are several references from the Gospel. If you take the time to look them up, you will see that Jesus gave thanks in everything — all things delivered, loaves of bread, the cup...and others around him also gave thanks.

- Matthew 11:25-26
- Matthew 15:36
- Mark 14:23
- Luke 22:17, 19
- John 6:11, 23; 11:41

In the Old Testament, Daniel was obedient to be thankful even when it was forbidden by the authorities. This shows that thankfulness must be a part of who you are right down to the core, unshakable even when being challenged in the toughest of circumstances:

> *Now when Daniel knew that the document was signed, he entered his house (now in his roof chamber he had windows open toward Jerusalem); and he continued kneeling on his knees three times a day, praying and giving thanks before his God, as he had been doing previously. Daniel 6:10*

According to the Bible, gratitude is a good thing

Psalms 92:1 states, *"It is a good thing to give thanks unto the Lord"*. As listed in the Bible, here are six reasons why we should be grateful:

1. Gratitude is a mighty tool in ushering us into the presence of God, which is necessary for personal strength and success.

   2 Chronicles 5:12, 13

   Psalms 95:2

   Psalms 100:4

Psalms 140:1

2. Gratitude causes us to abound in the faith, which is key to making things happen.

Colossians 2:7

3. Gratitude yields the peace of God in our hearts and minds.

Philippians 4:6, 7

4. Gratitude honors and magnifies God.

Psalms 50:23

Psalms 69:30

5. Gratitude is God's will.

Thessalonians 5:18

6. Gratitude is a good indicator of our spiritual condition.

Romans 1:21

Psalms 140:1

Thessalonians 1:2

1 Timothy 2:1

2 Timothy 1:3

Philemon 1:4

Psalms 109:30 (cp. Psalms 105:1, 2)

Psalms 111:1

So, when should we give thanks?

The Bible doesn't only tell us to give thanks, it tells us when, which can best be summarized in one word: always. Following, are four primary messages in the Bible regarding this issue and some relevant references:

1. In every circumstance

      Ephesians 5:20 (cp. Ephesians 1:16; 1 Thessalonians 1:2)

      Philippians 4:6

      Philippians 4:11

      1 Thessalonians 5:18

      2 Thessalonians 1:3; 2:13

2. Continually; habitually

      Ephesians 1:16; 5:20

      Philemon 1:4

      1 Thessalonians 1:2

      2 Timothy 1:3

      Hebrews 13:15 "

      Psalms 34:1; 35:28 (cp. 71:8)

3. Every morning and every evening

      1 Chronicles 23:30

4. Thank him daily

      Psalms 68:1

What should I be thankful for?

The wonderful thing about the Bible is that it provides complete instructions for everything that is asked of us. Now we know that we must be thankful, thereby showing gratitude for everything, and we also know when to be thankful. But the Bible does not stop there.

Here is what to be thankful for:

1. For his protection

      2 Samuel 22:49

2. For the wonders of creation and life (pretty much every detail of the day can fall into this category)

Psalms 139:14

3. For answered prayer

John 11:41

Most of all, a review of Bible versuses will tell you that the secret of maintaining a grateful heart is contentment. You can find specific references to this fact in   Philippians 4:11, 1 Timothy 6, and Hebrews 13:5, though the connection between contentment and gratefulness is made throughout the Bible.

Noah gives thanks

Most of us know the story of Noah and how he built an ark and sailed out the flood. But, do you know what Noah did first after the flood waters had subsided? That's right, he gave thanks to the Lord as detailed in the following verses from Genesis:

Then Noah built an altar to the LORD and, taking some of all the clean animals and clean birds, he sacrificed burnt offerings on it. 21 The LORD smelled the pleasing aroma and said in his heart: "Never again will I curse the ground because of man, even though [a] every inclination of his heart is evil from childhood. And never again will I destroy all living creatures, as I have done. "As long as the earth endures, seedtime and harvest, cold and heat, summer and winter, day and night will never cease." Genesis 8:20-22

Yes, building that altar to God and offering a sacrifice was giving thanks to the Lord. And through genuine gratitude, Noah found contentment and ultimately, success.

Bring the whole tithe into the storehouse, that there may be food in my house. Test me in this," says the LORD Almighty, "and see if I will not throw open the floodgates of heaven and pour out so much blessing that you will not have room enough for it. Malachi 3:10

SECTION II: Expressing Gratitude

Knowing the importance of gratitude, why we should show it, and when to give thanks is not enough if we don't know how to express it. Tithing is one of the best ways to show your gratitude to God and to the community in which you live, work, and attend religious services.

Whether you give to your church, a charity, a poor person, or to someone you love, your gift is a way of expressing gratitude. If your gift or tithe is not given in gratitude, then you shouldn't give it all. After all, what we are saying when we give our money and time is, "I have been blessed with enough wealth that I can give some to help others as my way of saying thanks." This is one reason why so many books on success teach tithing.

Tithing

Tithing has been practiced since early bible times. It is the concept that all people should praise and thank God through giving giving a portion of what it is that they have been given, whether it be money, time, crops, talents, or something else. Through giving, we have the opportunity to show real gratitude by offering some of our own resources in our thanksgiving -- through sacrifice, we show the depth of our feelings of thankfulness. According to several versus in 2 Corinthians, the principles of giving, or tithing, are as follows:

- Tithing is an investment the more we give, the more we will see in return.
- The amount you should tithe is personal -- give as you are able. If you are not giving from your heart, do not give at all. God is

only interested in genuine acts.

- Tithing is a form of prayer, thanksgiving, and gratitude.
- Tithing is a form of sharing, of giving back to others because you have been given so much.
- The act of tithing is in keeping with Jesus' example through his death, he gave the greatest gift of all. Our gifts demonstrate an acknowledgement of his sacrifice as we unselfishly give to others as he has given to us.

In every thing give thanks: for this is the will of God...
Thessalonians 5:18

The story of Job

You express gratitude when you are thankful and remain strong in times of strife. As I mentioned earlier, we all know that it is fairly easy to be grateful when times are good. But did you know that we should be grateful even when things are bad? Of course we should. Just because things are not currently going our way, doesn't mean that we shouldn't forget about all the great things that we have been given in our lives. This is true even if those good things are now gone. If you haven't already, pick up a Bible and

read the story of Job. I will give a summary here so that I can make a point:

> Job was a very, righteous man with God, and God rewarded him with wealth, and a large family. Then one day, God allowed Satan to take away all of Job's wealth, his children, and plagued him with boils and sores. Even still, Job did not question God. He had a very interesting conversation with God, and in the end, God restored Job's health, allowed him to live a long life, and gave him more wealth, and more children.

One of the themes of the story is that even though you are good, you may still suffer in life. One of the reasons why Job is my favorite book of the Bible is that there are many lessons to be learned from it. Many of us picture ourselves in Job's shoes, we feel like we are suffering for no reason. However, I doubt that most of us who feel that way have ever suffered anything like Job. I'm not trying to downplay any suffering you've had, but you should take a lesson from Job himself.

One of the lessons of Job is that suffering is part of our human experience. And, like Job, through suffering we can learn valuable lessons and come out successful. It doesn't say so in the Bible, but I believe that Job was grateful for his experience. Being a righteous man before and after his suffering, giving thanks to the Lord would be an everyday prayer for Job.

If you are suffering, or have suffered in the past, you may be saying, "I have nothing to be grateful for." Surely, I used to think that way...

My story

I feel it's important for you that I tell my story, because through it, you will see that I didn't come from a life of privilege and you will have a better understanding of what happened at my mother's death bed. You will see how I came to live a life of gratitude, even though it seems like I have very little to have been grateful for. In fact, what I am about to tell you will shock you.

I was born and raised in Warren, Ohio, a small steel mill town not far from

Youngstown, Ohio. My dad worked in a steel mill and my mom was a stay-at-home mom. I have two sisters, one older and one younger. My childhood and teenage years were full of pain, sadness, and fear. For you see, I am a survivor of child abuse. My childhood was very violent for my sisters and me. Being the only boy, I took most of the physical violence from both my father and mother. That's right, my mom was just as violent as my father. Granted, as I got older, my mom didn't physically attack me, but she would make sure that my dad did.

One of my earliest memories was a violent one. I was probably around four or five years old. I know that I wasn't in school yet, and that my older sister was at school. My dad came home from work and was going to make pancakes for me. At the time, pancakes were my favorite food. I liked them plain, without syrup.

Well, my dad came home and for some reason, he and my mom argued. I don't know about what, I was too small to comprehend. My dad started hitting my mom. He pinned her down and as he was beating on her, I picked up a baseball bat and started hitting him in the back. It didn't even get my dad's attention. I felt helpless. Then, I hit him right on the spine and he cringed. He stopped hitting my mom and went about his business. Not really a great first memory of your parents together.

So, you see that I didn't have a great childhood, in fact, I didn't even have a good childhood. I could have sat around and became a bitter, old fool. But, I didn't.

The abuse eventually turned to us kids. At times, the abuse would be pretty severe. There was also emotional abuse. We weren't allowed to have any friends. However, I did have my sisters. We had each other to help us through the terrible times. I am thankful for that. Because, if it wasn't for my sisters, I don't think I could have made it through the abuse or to even adjust to a normal adulthood.

This is one of those things that you don't really think about, but yes, I was very grateful to have had the sisters I did. Even though it was something terrible that brought us closer. I'm telling you this so that you can understand that I am someone who has come from a tough background and you would think that I wouldn't have anything to be thankful for. This was true in my early years as an adult. I wasn't thankful. I hated my life and I was very angry. Though I was smart enough to know that I wanted something better for myself, living in the shadow of my parents' abuse was hard.

I was able to work my way through college. I got jobs and finally married a lovely woman. In some ways, I was a success. However, I wanted more. I did all the right things -- I went to college and studied computers. But still, I had debt problems, and even in my 30's, I still didn't feel I was where I wanted to be.

My attitude was bitter. I was mad that I had to come so much farther than a normal person. I was mad my parents weren't rich. I was mad that they treated me so badly.

On my wedding day, my father died. At this time, I didn't have a good relationship with my parents, so I just thought of it as just another crappy thing to happen in my life. In the next year, my mom's health got worse. She had cancer, high blood pressure, diabetes, and failing kidneys. My parents weren't the healthiest people, and they died at a young age, both in their early 60's.

I want you to know what it was like leading up to my mom's death in the hospital. We knew my mom was going to die soon and we were just waiting for it to happen so that we could close that chapter in our lives. My mom was still clinging to material things -- not really caring or even being grateful of what we, especially my older sister, were doing for her. Now, when I say my mom was clinging to material things -- we are talking about a lot of junk, nothing of real value.

Well, finally my mom went into the hospital one last time. I traveled to be with my older sister and to help her out. My younger sister lives in New York City and it was impractical for her to come. Besides, there was no real love between us and our mom. I know that might sound cruel, but read on. Little did we know what was in store for us.

I believe that events happen for a reason. There are many reasons for what happened at my mom's death bed. There was a lot I learned from my mom in that last week. My mom knew she was dying and at first she tried to hide the fact. Then, for the first time, she expressed love for her children. She understood that her life wasn't about those things in her house, but about having people love you. She was grateful for the fact that we had tolerated her in the last years and that my sister and I would be with her until she passed away.

Not only did my mom learn about gratitude, but so did I. Since, she passed away, I have often reflected on that time and am still grateful that I had that experience. Through it, I was able to mend a lifetime of pain, anger, and bitterness with my mom and also with my dad.

In some odd way, I believe that my mom's life had lead up to this point just so she could learn a lesson. She was grateful to have been able to share her final days on earth with my sister and me. I'm grateful to her, too. And from that time on, I knew what I was missing in my life. Yes, you guessed it: gratitude. I looked at my life and said to myself, "...look at all the things that I have and that I have done. I have two wonderful sisters, a lovely wife, and I'm not living in a dumpster." It dawned on me that what was stopping me from reaching the success that I always wanted was my lack of gratitude. First, I needed to be grateful for the things that I had. Second, I need to be grateful for the things I wanted.

I always wanted to be an entrepreneur. So, that is what I pursued. Guess what happened? I meant a guy by the name of Matt Furey who was already a very successful entrepreneur and who was willing to help me. Through Matt's help, I was able to launch a successful web site for runners, www.runningtough.com. Now, how do you think this happened? I couldn't have done this even two years earlier. Yet in the prior two years, I didn't get smarter and I didn't go to school. In fact, I didn't even change jobs. Nothing about me changed except that I started to be grateful and started to believe in myself.

Like the saying goes, "when the student is ready, the teacher appears." I had not previously known who Matt Furey was, or that there were people out there that help other people to become successful. In fact, I had worked for a few millionaires and all of them were bitter, ungrateful, and never wanted to help others. Not only that, but Matt himself knew about gratitude. He helped me to refine my gratitude to make my business more successful. (See the section on business success.)

Be anxious for nothing; but in every thing by prayer and supplication (to ask for earnestly and humbly) with thanksgiving let your requests be made known unto God.
Philippians 4:6

SECTION III: What Others Say About Gratitude

I have dozens of success books in my personal library and I have read them all. Some have good advice and some, not so good. But, there is one thing missing in all of them: the issue of gratitude. There are a few books, like The Science of Getting Rich that do mention gratitude, but it is mostly in passing.

Books on success that talk about gratitude

Wayne Allyn Root wrote an interesting book, The Zen of Gambling. This book is about success in business and sports gambling. It is about taking risks in life and never giving up. He actually talks about the spiritual principles behind his success. In Chapter Nine of his book, Root spells out some rules of success. In Roots' rule #15, "Faith, Family and Freedom," he states the following:

"First of all, I thank God for all that I am, and all that I have achieved. I am a spiritual being. Without God I'd be nowhere. I give my goals, my ambitions, my worries, and all my many challenges to God. He takes the burden off my shoulders."

"Second, I thank God for my family. They are the foundation of my life. If you study super achievers, virtually all of them base their lives around their spouses and children." [3]

As I mentioned in the introduction of this book, in 1910, a gentleman by the name of Wallace Wattles, wrote The Science of Getting Rich. Wattles' book has taught me a lot about creating wealth and one of its secrets is the understanding of gratitude. Below is what Wallace has to say about gratitude. His words are in italics, and my comments are between brackets [].

Wallace is talking about conveying one's wants (of getting rich) to what he calls the Formless Substance. We can interpret this as God.

"... and you will see that in order to do so it becomes necessary to relate yourself to the Formless Intelligence in a harmonious way.

To secure this harmonious relation is a matter of such primary and vital importance that I shall give some space to its discussion here, and give you instructions which, if you will follow them, will be certain to bring you into perfect unity of mind with God.

The whole process of mental adjustment and atonement can be summed up in one word, gratitude.

First, you believe that there is one Intelligent Substance, from which all things proceed; second, you believe that this Substance gives you everything you desire; and third, you relate yourself to It by a feeling of deep and profound gratitude.

Many people who order their lives rightly in all other ways are kept in poverty by their lack of gratitude. Having received one gift from God,

---

[3] "The Zen of Gambling", Wayne Allyn Root, p.125

they cut the wires which connect them with Him by failing to make acknowledgment.

It is easy to understand that the nearer we live to the source of wealth, the more wealth we receive; and it is easy also to understand that the soul that is always grateful lives in closer touch with God than the one which never looks to Him in thankful acknowledgment.

The more gratefully we fix our minds on the Supreme when good things come to us, the more good things we will receive, and the more rapidly they will come; and the reason simply is that the mental attitude of gratitude draws the mind into closer touch with the source from which the blessings come.

If it is a new thought to you that gratitude brings your whole mind into closer harmony with the creative energies of the universe, consider it well, and you will see that it is true. The good things you already have come to you along the line of obedience to certain laws. Gratitude will lead your mind out along the ways by which things come; and it will keep you in close harmony with creative thought and prevent you from falling into competitive thought.

[Wallace is talking about two worldviews, one is where one believes that resources, i.e., riches are few and that people need to fight over them. This is the competitive thought. And, the other is that we live in a world of abundance, and that God will provide enough for everyone. This is the creative thought. So, many of us were brought up with the idea of money as a finite resource that you (and everyone else) need to compete for.]

Gratitude alone can keep you looking toward the All, and prevent you from falling into the error of thinking of the supply as limited; and to do that would be fatal to your hopes. There is a Law of Gratitude, and it is absolutely necessary that you should observe the law, if you are to get the results you seek. The law of gratitude is the natural principle that action and reaction are equal, and in opposite directions.

The grateful outreaching of your mind in thankful praise to the Supreme is a liberation or expenditure of force; it cannot fail to reach that to which it is addressed, and the reaction is an instantaneous movement toward you.

"Draw nigh unto God, and He will draw nigh unto you." That is a statement of psychological truth.

And if your gratitude is strong and constant, the reaction in Formless Substance will be strong and continuous; the movement of the things you want will be always toward you. Notice the grateful attitude that Jesus took; how He always seems to be saying, "I thank Thee, Father, that Thou hearest me." You cannot exercise much power without gratitude; for it is gratitude that keeps you connected with Power.

But the value of gratitude does not consist solely in getting you more blessings in the future. Without gratitude you cannot long keep from dissatisfied thought regarding things as they are. The moment you permit your mind to dwell with dissatisfaction upon things as they are, you begin to lose ground. You fix attention upon the common, the ordinary, the poor, and the squalid and mean; and your mind takes the form of these things. Then you will transmit these forms or mental images to the Formless, and the common, the poor, the squalid, and mean will come to you.

To permit your mind to dwell upon the inferior is to become inferior and to surround yourself with inferior things.

On the other hand, to fix your attention on the best is to surround yourself with the best, and to become the best. The Creative Power within us makes us into the image of that to which we give our attention.

We are Thinking Substance, and thinking substance always takes the form of that which it thinks about.

[When Wallace is talking about Thinking Substance, he is saying that we have the power to create through prayer.]

The grateful mind is constantly fixed upon the best; therefore it tends to become the best; it takes the form of character of the best, and will receive the best.

Also, faith is born of gratitude. The grateful mind continually expects good things, and expectation becomes faith. The reaction of gratitude upon one's own mind produces faith; and every outgoing wave of grateful thanksgiving increases faith. He who has no feeling of gratitude cannot long retain a living faith; and without a living faith you cannot get rich by the creative method, as we shall see in the following chapters.

It is necessary, then, to cultivate the habit of being grateful for every good thing that comes to you; and to give thanks continuously. And because all things have contributed to your advancement, you should include all things in your gratitude.

Do not waste time thinking or talking about the shortcomings or wrong actions of plutocrats or trust magnates. Their organization of the world has made your opportunity; all you get really comes to you because of them.

Do not rage against corrupt politicians; if it were not for politicians we should fall into anarchy, and your opportunity would be greatly lessened.

God has worked a long time and very patiently to bring us up to where we are in industry and government, and He is going right on with His work. There is not the least doubt that He will do away with plutocrats, trust magnates, captains of industry, and politicians as soon as they can be spared; but in the meantime, behold they are all very good. Remember that they are all helping to arrange the lines of transmission along with your riches will come to you, and be grateful to them all. This will bring you into harmonious relations with the good in everything, and the good in everything will move toward you.

Most people think that capitalism is about taking away resources from someone else, that it is sort of a dog-eat-dog world. But, as Wallace has pointed out, it doesn't have to be that way.

Sure, you can go and do things that win you money by taking it away from someone else. This is what Wallace calls "competitive thought." But, in the long run, you won't really win because if you can take it away, someone can take it away from you. You will end up spending so much of your time trying to defend it that you will find yourself tired and bitter. But, when you follow the "Creative Way," and give thanks for your business and that we truly do live in a world of abundance, then this is true capitalism.

These are powerful words, and so true. In fact, I think you should read them again.

*Learn to cultivate a feeling of gratitude. It is hard to
have negative feelings if you have an
inner feeling of
gratitude.*

SECTION IV: Gratitude and Business Success

In this section, I will talk about gratitude that makes you successful and some practical things that you can do.

Wallace has some very wise business advice. This advice works well for giving customers more in use value than they pay in cash value. This is a great way to be grateful towards your customers and it will make them grateful (and faithful) to you. Let me tell you, this is some of the best business advice that I have ever heard. Plus, it is a moral and ethical way to run a business. Below is what Wallace has to say about use value vs. cash value. His words are in italics, and my comments are between brackets [].

> [In your business dealings you] *do not need to deal with others unfairly; you do not have to get something for nothing, but can give to every person more than you take from them.*

> *You cannot give every person more in cash market value than you take from them, but you can give them more in use value than the case value of the thing you take from them. The paper, ink, and other material in this book may not be worth the money you paid for it, but if the ideas suggested by it bring you thousands of dollars, you have not been wronged by those who sold it to you; they have given you a great use value for a small cash value.*

> *Let us suppose that I own a picture by one of the great artists, which, in any civilized community, is worth thousands of dollars. I take it to Baffin Bay, and by "salesmanship" induce an Eskimo to give a bundle*

of furs worth $500 for it. I have really wronged him, for he has no use for the picture; it has no use value for him; it will not add to his life.

But suppose I give him a gun worth $50 for his furs; then he has made a good bargain. He has use for the gun; it will get him many more furs and much food; it will add to his life in every way; it will make him rich.

When you rise from the competitive to the creative plane, you can scan your business transactions very strictly, and if you are selling any man anything which does not add more to his life than the thing he gives you in exchange, you can afford to stop it. You do not have to beat anybody in business. And if you are in a business which does beat people, get out of it at once.

Give every person more in use value than you take from them in cash value; then you are adding to the life of the world by every business transaction.

If you have people working for you, you must take from them more in cash value than you pay them in wages; but you can so organize your business that it will be filled with the principle of advancement, and so that each employee who wishes to do so may advance a little every day.

You can make your business do for your employees that this book is doing for you. You can so conduct your business that it will be a sort of ladder, by which every employee who will take the trouble may climb to riches themselves; and given the opportunity, if they will not do so it is not your fault.

And finally, because you are to cause the creation of your riches from

Formless Substance [God] which permeates all your environment, it does not follow that they are to take shape from the atmosphere and come into being before your eyes.

If you want a [computer], for instance, I do not mean to tell you that you are to impress the thought of a [computer] on Thinking Substance until the [computer] is formed without hands, in the room where you sit, or elsewhere. But if you want a [computer], hold the mental image of it with the most positive certainty that it is being made, or is on its way to you. After once forming the thought, have the most absolute and unquestioning faith that the [computer] is coming; never think of it, or speak of it, in any other way than as being sure to arrive. Claim it as already yours.

[Another key to success is that while you are thinking of the object you want, in this case the computer, you should also thank God for it in advance. I will talk more about this in the next section.]

It will be brought to you by the power of the Supreme Intelligence, acting upon the minds of men. If you live in Maine, it may be that a man will be brought from Texas or Japan to engage in some transaction which will result in your getting what you want.

If so, the whole matter will be as much to that man's advantage as it is to yours.

Do not forget for a moment that the Thinking Substance is through all, in all, communicating with all, and can influence all. The desire of Thinking Substance for fuller life and better living has caused the creation of all the [computers] already made; and it can cause the creation of millions more, and will, whenever someone sets it in motion by desire and faith, and by acting in a Certain Way [The way taught in "The Science of Getting Rich"].

You can certainly have a [computer] in your house; and it is just as certain that you can have any other thing or things which you want, and which you will use for the advancement of your own life and the lives of others.

You need not hesitate about asking largely; "it is your Father's pleasure to give you the kingdom," said Jesus.

[God] wants to live all that is possible in you, and wants you to have all that you can or will use for the living of the most abundant life.

If you fix upon your consciousness the fact that the desire you feel for the possession of riches is one with the desire of Omnipotence for more complete expression, your faith becomes invincible.

Once I saw a little boy sitting at a piano, and vainly trying to bring harmony out of the keys; and I saw that he was grieved and provoked by his inability to play real music. I asked him the cause of his aggravation, and he answered, "I can feel the music in me, but I cannot make my hands go right." The music in him was the URGE of Original Substance, containing all the possibilities of all life; all that there is of music was seeking expression through the child.

God, the One Substance, is trying to live and do and enjoy things through humanity. He is saying, "I want hands to build wonderful structures, to play divine harmonies, to paint glorious pictures; I want feet to run my errands, eyes to see my beauties, tongues to tell mighty truths and to sing marvelous songs," and so on.

All that there is of possibility is seeking expression through men. God wants those who can play music to have pianos and every other instrument, and to have the means to cultivate their talents to the fullest extent; He wants those who can appreciate beauty to be able to surround themselves with beautiful things; He wants those who can discern truth to have every opportunity to travel and observe; He wants those who can appreciate dress to be beautifully clothed, and those who can appreciate good food to be luxuriously fed.

He wants all these things because it is Himself that enjoys and appreciates them; it is God who wants to play, and sing, and enjoy beauty, and proclaim truth, and wear fine clothes, and eat good foods.

"It is God that worketh in you to will and to do," said Paul.

The desire you feel for riches is the Infinite, seeking to express Himself in you as He sought to find expression in the little boy at the piano.

So you need not hesitate to ask largely.

Your part is to focalize and express the desires of God.

This is a difficult point with most people; they retain something of the old idea that poverty and self-sacrifice are pleasing to God. They look upon poverty as a part of the plan, a necessity of nature. They have the idea that God has finished His work, and made all that He can make, and that the majority of men must stay poor because there is not enough to go around. They hold to so much of this erroneous thought that they feel ashamed to ask for wealth; they try not to want more than a very modest competence, just enough to make them fairly comfortable.

I recall now the case of one student who was told that he must get in his mind a clear picture of the things he desired, so that the creative thought of them might be impressed on the Formless Substance. He was a very poor man, living in a rented house, and having only what he earned from day to day; and he could not grasp the fact that all wealth was his. So, after thinking the matter over, he decided that he might reasonably ask for a new rug for the floor of his best room, and an anthracite coal stove to heat the house during the cold weather. Following the instructions given in this book, he obtained these things in a few months; and then it dawned upon him that he had not asked enough. He went through the house in which he lived, and planned all the improvements he would like to make in it; he mentally added a bay window here and a room there, until it was complete in his mind as his ideal home; and then he planned its furnishings.

Holding the whole picture in his mind, he began living in the Certain Way, and moving toward what he wanted; and he owns the house now, and is rebuilding it after the form of his mental image. And now, with still larger faith, he is going on to get greater things. It has been unto him according to his faith, and it is so with you and with all of us.

Giving thanks in advance

Remember what was said in a preceding chapter about gratitude: be as thankful for it all the time as you expect to be when it has taken form. The person who can sincerely thank God for the things which as yet they own only in imagination, has real faith. They will get rich; they will cause the creation of whatsoever they want.

Whenever you get checks in the mail from customers or receive orders, you should gives thanks to God, or the universe. You should check your bank accounts everyday, and gives thanks.

Thanking Customers

Unfortunately, most business just give lip service to the idea of showing gratitude to customers. Have you ever been to a store and after you check out, they say "thank you for shopping at our store." Call customer support on the phone and before you hang up, they'll likely say "thank you for using our service." In fact, this statement is printed on most receipts. But, when was the last time that you really felt appreciated when hearing one of these comments?

You know that most clerks and phone representatives are all trained to say "thank you." They say it so many times a day that it loses all meaning. Even if you run into someone, like a manager or even the store owner, who does mean it when they say "thanks", the word is so over-used that it has become meaningless. It is a rare store that goes out of its way to really help you and to show you real gratitude.

Do you know what? When I do experience genuine gratitude, I go back to those stores over and over, even if they do not have the best prices. I tell people that I know to shop there. If they say that someone else has a better price, I always say the service is better at my recommended store.

Real gratitude can give you an edge over your competition

If you own a business or are thinking of starting one, this is where real gratitude can really pay off and give you a competitive edge over your competition.

In the previous section, we read Wallace's advice on giving customers more in use value than in cash value. This is a great way of showing gratitude towards your customers. Plus, they will feel grateful towards you because they received something worth more than they paid. You can see the two-way street here: customers are more likely to buy from you again if you are genuinely grateful for their business. And, if they feel grateful for the value they received from you, they will want to give you more business, either from themselves or by recommending your product or service to others. It is a win-win situation. I do not understand why businesses do not do this more often.

You may be asking, "how can I give customers more in use value than in cash value? Let's look at the example that Wallace used with the Eskimo. That is, you sell a gun to an Eskimo who hunts for a living for $50. That Eskimo now has a tool that will help him to hunt more effectively. And over the course of a year, he can easily make ten times or more what he paid for the gun.

This concept still works in many ways today. If I told you that if you pay me $5,000, I would show you how you can make $50,000 over the next year, would you think that would be a good investment? Why wouldn't you buy my consulting services, particularly if I guaranteed the results? Would you not be calling me up after a year and thanking me? You bet you would.

So, if you can sell your customers something that makes them more money, saves them more money, or gives them more enjoyment of something than they would otherwise get from it, then that is a great way to show gratitude. The good news is that most businesses can provide this product or service. If you haven't done this, you haven't tried hard enough to think about telling your potential customers about how your product or service will give them more use value, or you haven't thought of a new product or service to offer your prospects that will.

You can offer your customers something very direct, like a consulting service that will increase their revenues or teach them to market their product or services better. Or, you can tell them how to save money by reducing expenses. Does your product save time? Does it allow your customers to enjoy something more?

If you have racked your brain and still can't think of a way to show your customers that your product or service has more use value than your competitors, then give them more!

Adding use value to your product or service

These are called *premiums*. Don't just sell a widget, give customers a free book on how to use the widget, offer them a video that will show them the many uses of the widget, offer them a free consultation on how to maximize the widget, or provide free installation. Or, implement a "buy one and get one free" program. You, of course, need to make sure that the price of your product or service covers any additional premiums you are going to include. But, usually when you give customers a premium that provides use value, it doesn't usually cost much to produce. The cost of creating an e-book on the use of your widget is virtually nil. Even a paper version can be quite inexpensive to produce in bulk.

Another way to show that you value your customers and to express your gratitude for their business is to offer sales and discounts to those you keep seeing again and again. Imagine opening your mailbox and finding an exclusive discount. Would you feel special? Of course you would. Everyone likes to feel appreciated and most like to be a part of an elite group. And that is exactly what loyal customers are.

Through sales and discounts targeted only to your repeat customers, I guarantee that you'll not only keep your regulars coming back, but you'll gain new ones as well. How could you earn new customers simply by showing gratitude to those who already purchase your products or services? It is called "word-of-mouth." People talk. And since being appreciated is so rare in today's world, your discount or sale will give them something to talk about. But don't make the mistake of trying to fake your gratitude just to get new business. Your gratitude must be genuine and your offers must be extended in thanks, otherwise you'll get nowhere. Most people are smart enough to figure out your motives.

Testimonials are your customers' way of showing gratitude to you. (This is also a way for you to express gratitude to a business whose product or service you have bought.) When you receive a testimonial, you should of course be grateful for it, because it shows that your product or service is truly helping people. You should display it or put it up on your web site.

This shows gratitude to your customer. You'll find that people usually like to have their name up somewhere and to be associated with you, your product, or service.

Thank your employees

Once again, most companies pay lip service to showing their employees gratitude. This is wrong. After all, these are the people who are building your business. Again, Wallace has some good advice about how to show gratitude towards your employees:

> *If you have people working for you, you must take from them more in cash value than you pay them in wages; but you can so organize your business that it will be filled with the principle of advancement, and so that each employee who wishes to do so may advance a little every day.*

> *You can make your business do for your employees that this book is doing for you. You can so conduct your business that it will be a sort of ladder, by which every employee who will take the trouble may climb to riches themselves; and given the opportunity, if they will not do so it is not your fault.*

Extend employee to employee gratitude

If you are an employee, don't forget to show gratitude to those you work with. You cannot get your job done without help, and most of us tend to take people from granted once we have worked with them for awhile. We come to expect people to do things the really don't have to do, such running interference with co-workers, helping with work back-ups, or even grabbing some lunch for us while they are out.

Anything that someone does for you that goes beyond their job description should be met with a genuine "thank you." Does that mean that you shouldn't thank people who a just doing their jobs? Of course not, sometimes they are the one who need to hear it most. And don't forget about your supervisors and managers, send a note to someone in leadership who has gone out of their way to help you at work.

Blessed be the Lord, who daily loadeth us with benefits..
Psalms 68:19

SECTION V: How to Show Gratitude

In various sections throughout this book, I have discussed the ways to show gratitude. In this section, I will summarize the various ways to say "thanks."

Following, are six easy ways to say thank you to those around you:

1. <u>Prayer</u> - Gratitude should be first said in a prayer. Thank God for all you have been given, for those who are in your life, and for all of your success. Pray prayers of thanks even for the bad things that happen, for the lessons learned are of true value and ultimately enhance your life. Show gratitude for others by praying for them in the same way you would pray for yourself.

2. <u>A simple note or testimonial</u> Write a note even if you don't send the note. This is a good way to pray and to thank people you can no longer find or who have passed away. Back when I was in therapy for my abuse, I was asked to write a letter to my parents. At the time, my parents were alive. The letter was filled with a lot of negative emotions — a lot of hate. The sole purpose of the letter was to get all of these emotions out.

Since, that time, I have forgiven my parents, who are both dead now. Because of the incredible event that happened at my mom's death bed, I am very grateful for that event and that both my mom and dad have redeemed themselves. I have written a new letter to them, this one is about gratitude.

3. <u>Use value</u> Offer more than is expected. People aren't used to getting more than they pay for. There is no better way to thank your customers for their business than to somehow enhance an element of their lives.

4. <u>A return favor</u> If someone does a favor for you, return it as quickly as possible. Simply stating, "I owe you one" is as worthwhile as a hollow "thank you." You will shock people (in a good way) when you actually do show your gratitude with action.

5. <u>A genuine feeling</u> Don't just say thanks, mean it. How can you demonstrate that you really mean it? Look the recipient of your "thank you" in the eye, take their hand as you speak, or give a hearty hug along with your words. Tell the person why you are thankful. Instead of simply saying two words (thank you), say several. For example, instead of "thank you," say "thank you for being there for me — I could not have come through this without you. You brought a warmness into my house each time you stepped through the door."

6. <u>A gift in return</u> (also money given)— Again, if you are going to reciprocate a gift or a favor, act quickly or the meaning will be lost.

Mistakes

Sometimes in the effort to get it right, we can make mistakes in the way we show our gratitude. Following, are three mistakes to avoid:

1. <u>Going overboard</u> - You don't need to thank everyone for every little thing they do for you every day or you will drive yourself, and them, batty. And, don't go overboard thanking one person. The gratitude shown should be equal to what was done.

2. <u>Being too modest</u> - When accepting gratitude, don't be too modest and accept the thanks given, even if it is a gift.

3. <u>Confusing gratitude with acceptance of a less than desirable experience</u> - The desire to express gratitude should not replace your strength.

Here are some other general Dos for showing gratitude:

Gratitude Do's

- Thank the higher power.
- Thank the people who you love.
- Thank the people who help you.
- Thank the people in your everyday life.
- Thank people when they do things for you.
- Give thanks everyday.
- Accept gratitude.

Visualization is the key

I will give thanks to the Lord with all my heart; I will tell of all thy wonders. Psalms 9:1

Visualization is imagining an image in your mind. Sometimes this will be a moving image. The reason for visualization is that it helps you to get into the right frame of mind before you express your gratitude. We actually do naturally think in pictures, but some people have a hard time with visualization. This chapter will help you with your visualization. With your package, I have included several items with pictures on them that will help you to visualize.

The secret to gratitude towards God is to put real feeling into it -- not just to say the words like some empty prayer. For gratitude to work, or for that matter for prayer to work, you have to be sincere and to have a real feeling for it. The phrase, "with all my heart," means with feeling, not just saying the words.

One of the secrets to prayer is that gratitude is said first

A visualization can help put you into the correct frame of mind before expressing gratitude. Here is an example you can use to get the right feeling for expressing thankfulness for your spouse:

Imagine that your spouse is away on a business trip in a city close to home, however, they had chosen to fly since it was quicker. In the morning, your spouse calls you and tells you that he or she will be home by 5:00 PM. No big deal, in fact, you may be wondering what's going to be for dinner or you may be waiting to discuss some bill with your spouse. You go about your daily business and then turn on the television.

"We interrupt this program to bring you news of a terrible disaster. There has been a plane crash, we have sketchy details at this time. However, it was flight 387, coming from..."

"Oh my gosh", you say to yourself, as a sense of panic overcomes you. That's the flight your spouse was to be on.

Just then the phone rings and you get that sinking feeling. Is this the airline calling me to tell me the bad news? You pick up the phone, your hands trembling so badly that you can hardly hold the receiver.

You hear the voice of your spouse. "Thank God you are alright," you say.

"Where are you? Aren't you on that flight?"

Your spouse tells you that they were delayed in traffic and as a result, the flight was missed. Due to the crash and the airport being so close, your spouse decides to drive the few hours it takes to get home.

You can't wait until your spouse gets home so that you can hold him/her in your arms. You had thought you had lost your spouse and now you know that everything is okay. You want to tell you spouse that you love him/her so very much.

You hear a car pull up, you look out the window -- it's your loved one. You run to the door and grab your spouse and give him/her a hug. You never want to let go. Through this experience, you have realized how grateful you are to have him/her in your life.

That is the feeling you need to have when you say thanks to God for your wife, husband, children, and other loved ones.

You can also do shorter visualizations, such as closing your eyes and imagining what someone might have been like as a small child. For example, if you have a parent who at times is hard to deal with, think about him or her as a child. What were her hopes and dreams? What might have made him sad? What failed him/ her to make him/her the person you know today? Through visualizing the person in the past, asking some important questions, and "seeing" them as a fragile human being, you can feel the compassion that sometimes must come before genuine gratitude is felt.

The secret to gratitude is the sincere feeling you put into it

When you do this, your relationship will change. Imagine being excited when your spouse comes home. If you have been in a relationship for any length of time, I'm sure you have let this slip.

Some of you might think that this is extreme or silly. But, I wouldn't be telling you this if it weren't important. You need to be grateful for the things and the people you have while you still have them, not when you don't. Otherwise, when something bad does happen, you will be left full of regret. Plus, God isn't going to help you if you aren't grateful for the things that he has given you. You can't take your spouse for granted. What happens if one day he or she gets cancer and you want to pray to God to cure the cancer? Why would God answer your prayer? You never thanked him for what you had. As Job said, *The Lord gave and the Lord has taken away* (Job 1:21).

That is why every prayer should always start with thanks and gratitude. If you have nothing to ask for, you should pray anyway and give thanks.

When you are grateful for someone, you will appreciate him/her more and grow closer together. I realized this in my own relationship with my wife Kim. We weren't having any trouble or anything. But, after we had been married for a few years, things started to become "just everyday." Like, "Oh, Kim's home, I wonder what's for dinner."

Once I started to give thanks to the Almighty for her, things changed. I did get excited when she came home or when I came home. Our relationship just improved. At the time, I hadn't even told her personally how much I was grateful for her. Now that is a separate topic, but it can improve your relationships even more. Things that you are grateful for, you seem to take care of more.

*And that bringeth me forth from mine enemies:
thou also hast lifted me up on high above them that rose up
against me: thou hast delivered me from the violent man.*
2 Samuel 22:49

SECTION VI: The Gratitude Prayer

Before you pray this prayer, please read the section on visualization and on how to feel gratitude. If you do, you will get more out of this prayer:

1. Thank you Lord for my life, my health, my wife/husband, my wife/husband's health, my house, my wealth, and my business.

2. I'm sorry that my thoughts, words, deeds and actions are not always pure, kind, and good.

3. Lord, I need your help to protect me and I need your forgiveness. Please enter into my body so that I may see the world as you see it.

Let's look at each of these parts in more detail

1. Thank you Lord for my life, my health, my wife/husband, my wife/husband's health, my house, my wealth, and my business.

> *You notice that the prayer starts out with gratitude. This is important.*

> *You always start with your own life because you have been given the gift of life.*

To get the proper feeling, think of how you would feel if you were told you had five days to live, then later told that there was a mistake and that there is nothing wrong with you. How grateful would you be for your life?
You then give thanks for your own health.

When I thank God for my wife, Kim, I picture her inside my head. I get the feeling I describe in "How to Feel Grateful."

2. I'm sorry that my thoughts, words, deeds and actions are not always pure, kind, and good.

You should think of the thoughts, words and deeds that you have said and done over the past day and in the longer past.

3. Lord, I need your help to protect me and I need your forgiveness. Please come enter into my body so that I may see the world as you see it.

Here is a great visualization: you picture a golden road that goes up at a 45 degree angle. It goes up into the sky or into the clouds. This road leads to heaven, so it goes on for quite a while.

Standing on the road close to where the road meets the ground, is the Lord. (See below on how you can visualize him.) Then, you picture yourself at around the age of 10, running up the road toward the Lord. The Lord bends down as you run into his open arms. He hugs you to show you his love and also to protect you.

Then, I picture my 10- year- old self pointing back at me, and then he takes the Lord's hand and leads him toward my adult self. When Jesus is right in front of me, I then ask him to enter into me. This completes your prayer.

Visualization for The Gratitude Prayer

When I pray, it helps me when I picture an imagine of Jesus. However, you can picture God the Father, or any other God or figure that you feel most comfortable with. For all visualization, you want as much detail as possible. It may help to write down as many details that you can. For instance, here is a good exercise to get down the vision of the Lord:

I stand up, I don't close my eyes, but you can if it will help to do the visualization better. I picture Jesus standing in front of me. He is wearing a white robe that goes all the way down to His ankles. He is wearing brown sandals. He has his hands down by his side, he has brown hair, and a brown beard. He is smiling at me, and there is a glow around his head. His smile is warm and it shows that he loves me very much. I could almost cry from his love. I then ask him to enter into my body, so that he may show me how he sees the world. He then turns around, and enters into my body.

Don't worry if your description doesn't match to that of any real historical person, or is even a real person, if you choose some other religious icon. Your vision doesn't have to match anyone else's either.

When to Say the Gratitude Prayer

You need to be grateful repeatedly for the things you have and want. You need to do it once daily at the minimum. Pick a special, pre-determined time to awake in the morning and train spiritually. Give thanks, say you are sorry, ask for forgiveness, and ask for help. Walk the golden road which leads to the arms of God until you see and feel a closeness and warmth that is beyond normal feeling. See the Lord enter you, turn around inside of you and look out your eyes so you can see the world as the Lord sees it. Say one good prayer all day long every day.

Do the most you can with what you have to promote the well-being of all mankind all over the world.

The best time to say this prayer is in the morning. However, it should be done throughout the day. What I do, is to pray the prayer in detail in the morning. Then, throughout the day, I pray a shorter version of it, making sure I feel each emotion, gratitude, sorrow, and help.

If you have trouble remembering to do the prayer in the morning, you can order a the poster that goes with this book and place it out somewhere where you will see it when you first get up. Hang it over your bed, in the bathroom, or on the inside of your door, so that you will see it before you leave for work in the morning. The poster can be used as both a reminder and to help with visualization.

You should start to feel uncomfortable starting your day, without doing the prayer. Why would you want to start a day off without giving thanks for it? Each day is a gift. All the things you will experience in that day are also a gifts.

Another way to help you give thanks throughout the day is to use the magnets that I also designed for this book. Place them in the places where you will be. In the car, at work, in the kitchen, in the bathroom -- anywhere is fine as long as you will see them throughout your day. Wallace says the following about gratitude and prayer:

> *You do not show gratitude by repeating strings of words; you do it by holding the feeling of gratitude with unshakable purpose to attain it, and this is what gives you faith.*
>
> *The answer to prayer is not according to your faith while you are talking, but according to your faith while you are working.*

You cannot impress the mind of God by having a special Sabbath day set apart to tell Him what you want, and then forgetting Him during the rest of the week. You cannot impress Him by having special hours to go into your closet and pray, if you then dismiss the matter from your mind until the hour of prayer comes again.

Oral prayer is well enough, and has its effect, especially upon yourself, in clarifying your vision and strengthening your faith; but it is not your oral petitions which get you what you want. In order to become successful you do not need a "sweet hour of prayer" nor do you need to "pray without ceasing". But, you do need to be thankful throughout the day.

*I will give thanks to Thee, for I am fearfully
and wonderfully made; wonderful are thy works...*
Psalms 139:14

Final Thoughts

In this book, you have learned how the missing success link, gratitude, can turn things around for you. You now know where gratitude comes from, why it is important, how to express it, how to pray with it, and how to integrate it into both your professional and personal life. Take time to reflect on what you have learned and then put it to use.

We have all heard the phrase, "stop and smell the roses." This usually means to slow down, take a break, and look at the world around you. When you do this, you should develop a heightened appreciation for life. When you then give thanks for the world, it is even better.

So, I say "**stop and smell the roses and give thanks for them.**" Because, this makes life more enjoyable. At first, it may seem silly. But after a while, you get a wonderful feeling inside you.

Look at the sky each and every day, and whether it's blue, cloudy, or raining, give thanks. Give thanks for all the people around you, the birds chirping -- everything. When you do this, life will become more enjoyable.

What about when bad things happen?

Read the story of Job.

A lot of bad things happened to me. And, some are so bad, that you would think that there is no way I could ever be grateful. Yes, I felt that way as a teenager and also as a young adult. I was mad at everything and everyone. I wouldn't talk to people because I hated them. I hated God, too.

But, you know that there a lots and lots of people out there who have had bad things happen and, in the long run, things worked out. People have been fired and they end up doing something better with higher pay.

I'll give you a business example from my own experience:

It seemed that I had always attracted negative people. I had more than my share of crappy bosses, co-workers, and customers. It used to make me so mad. What did this make me do? It made me switch jobs to try and get away from the negative people -- only to run into more of them. Now, I didn't job hop or anything. I usually stayed on a job for a few years.

But, the positive things from this are:

- I received good raises each time I switched jobs.
- I gained more experience in switching jobs.
- I met more people (good ones).
- I learned to deal with difficult people.

If my first job would have been a nice place to work, perhaps I would have just stayed there my entire life and not grown. But for me, I needed to grow and these obstacles were thrown in my way so that I *could grow*. This doesn't mean that if you have been working at the same place all your life that you should quit and go somewhere else. If you are happy there, then your lessons lie in other experiences.

So, when faced with a negative boss or co-worker, consider that it might be a sign, telling you something that you really need to know — that you should move on, do that traveling you always wanted to do, or deal with a problem you've been avoiding. When you find the answer, you should be grateful for it.

When I started my running site, www.runningtough.com, guess what happened? I got some negative customers and people who weren't customers, who just attacked me. The dealing with difficult people in my jobs, helped me to deal with them again in the business world. Once again I was tested to deal with difficult people. If I didn't have experience in dealing with negative people, I would have quit my new venture and never involved myself in another business after the first time someone criticized me. So, I was grateful that I had had this practice. It doesn't bother me now. In fact, sometimes I think it is funny and other times I think it is sad because the people doing the criticizing are actually unhappy, ungrateful people.

When I was at my mom's side when she was dying, I kept a dairy for that week. One of the things I wrote in it was that I hoped my mom would be able to look back into this world and see how beautiful it all is, because then she can appreciate the experiences she had and the people who love her.

When we start looking at life and up to a higher power, we become more aware of how wonderful it all is. We don't need to wait until we die to see this, like my mom did. We shouldn't. Life is scary, but we can't live our life in fear. That is what my mom did. I realized that she did live her life in fear. She was afraid that people were going to hurt her, that life was going to disappoint her and she was afraid of dying.

She didn't give thanks for the wonderful things she had in life. If she did, she would have had more great things happen and the possibility of death wouldn't have been so scary. Sure, we are all afraid of death to some degree. That is why you need to realize that life itself is a gift -- a wonderful gift. You should be grateful for that gift. Because, the more gratitude you show the more of that gift you get. The better it becomes.

Gratitude will make you cease regretting life and blaming your problems on others. You stop dreaming of a better life and instead give thanks for it. When you are truly hungry is when you are the most thankful to have food. When you approach life in this way, and imagine your life without the things that you hold dear, then you can truly be grateful for them. You will look at the sun rise in the morning, and the sun set in the evening, and understand for the first time how wonderful it all is and you will truly be grateful.

Gratitude for your life is the most precious gift you can show, to your loved ones, to the universe and to God.

Thank you for reading this book. I hope you live a wonderful and grateful life.

Live in joy and gratitude.

Tohamas Brewster graduate of Kendall College of Art and Design has been a professional illustrator for the past 15 years. He now lives in Seattle Washington where he works as an Illustrator for his own design company Spatt Bolony.

Contact info: tohamas@spattbolony.com

For more information please visit:

www.thepowerofgratitude.com

Made in the USA